CONTENTS

CHOICE

Bhanu Kapil • *How to Wash a Heart* • Pavilion Poetry

RECOMMENDATIONS

Natalie Diaz • *Postcolonial Love Poem* • Faber
Ella Frears • *Shine, Darling* • Offord Road Books
Seán Hewitt • *Tongues of Fire* • Cape
Ranjit Hoskote • *The Atlas of Lost Beliefs* • Arc

SPECIAL COMMENDATION

Grace Nichols • *Passport to Here and There* • Bloodaxe

RECOMMENDED TRANSLATION

The Sea Needs No Ornament • Peepal Tree Press
Edited and translated by Loretta Collins Klobah and Maria Grau Perejoan

PAMPHLET CHOICE

Alycia Pirmohamed • *Hinge* • ignition press

WILD CARD

Wayne Holloway-Smith • *Love Minus Love* • Bloodaxe

REVIEWS
LISTINGS

Poetry Book Society

CHOICE SELECTORS RECOMMENDATION SPECIAL COMMENDATION	SANDEEP PARMAR & ANDREW McMILLAN
TRANSLATION SELECTOR	ILYA KAMINSKY
PAMPHLET SELECTORS	MARY JEAN CHAN & NICK MAKOHA
WILD CARD SELECTOR	ANTHONY ANAXAGOROU
CONTRIBUTORS	SOPHIE O'NEILL NATHANIEL SPAIN
EDITORIAL & DESIGN	ALICE KATE MULLEN

Main Membership Options

Choice
4 Books a Year: 4 Choice books & 4 *Bulletins* a year (UK £55, Europe £65, ROW £75)

World
8 Books: 4 Choices, 4 Translation books & 4 *Bulletins* (£98, £120, £132)

Charter
20 Books: 4 Choices, 16 Recommendations and 4 *Bulletins* (£180, £210, £235)

Complete
24 Books: 4 Choices, 16 Recommendations, 4 Translations, 4 *Bulletins* (£223, £265, £292)

Single copies of the *Bulletin* £9.99

Cover Art: Jiroe, Unsplash

Copyright Poetry Book Society and contributors. All rights reserved.
ISBN 9781913129187 ISSN 0551-1690

Poetry Book Society | Milburn House | Dean Street | Newcastle upon Tyne | NE1 1LF
0191 230 8100 | enquiries@poetrybooksociety.co.uk

WWW.POETRYBOOKS.CO.UK

LETTER FROM THE PBS

Usually some sort of theme or connection appears from our selections, but in this quarter no link (aside from brilliance) has jumped out at me. Maybe that is perfect for the current climate, something completely different on every page. We're delighted to announce Bhanu Kapil's "brilliantly relentless" *How to Wash a Heart* as our Summer Choice and we hope you will enjoy this and the other selections as much as we have.

We're extremely grateful for the support that our members and the wider poetry community have shown over the past few months. Despite these precarious times, perhaps unsurprisingly to PBS members who understand the power of poetry, there has been an upsurge in poetry book sales which has significantly helped our publishers and poets. Since the 14th of March, we've posted a daily poem on social media (@poetrybooksoc) to help you #keepcalmandreadpoems. As I write, Andrew McMillan is dusting down his laptop and preparing for our first ever PBS online book club on our Summer Recommendation *Tongues of Fire*. This will air on Instagram Live (@poetrybooksociety) on the 6th of May and will be available afterwards on our website. If you need any help accessing this and future episodes, please get in touch.

Please do remember we also offer gift memberships and can post books to your friends and family in isolation. Perhaps not quite as quickly as usual, but all orders are being supplied! Our PBS and Mslexia Pamphlet prize-winner, *Bloodlines* by Sarah Wimbush, is now available to order too. "I fell in love with the gusto, the sheer gritty texture of these poems," Amy Wack, judge.

We are delighted most publishers have kept to their original publication schedules, so we have been able to produce this *Bulletin* and supply your quarterly mailing. However, there have, understandably, been a few delayed publication dates. We have endeavoured to review titles that are available, but a couple of our recommendations have slipped to later in the year, so Charter and Complete members will receive Natalie Diaz's *Postcolonial Love Poem* in a separate later mailing. You can also pre-order all forthcoming books and we'll ensure you receive them as soon as possible.

We hope you are all staying safe and well. Thanks once again for your support and we hope this poetry parcel brings you some joy, solace and much-needed normality.

SOPHIE O'NEILL
PBS & INPRESS DIRECTOR

BHANU KAPIL

Bhanu Kapil is the author of five full-length books of poetry/prose: *The Vertical Interrogation of Strangers* (Kelsey Street Press, 2001), *Incubation: a space for monsters* (Leon Works, 2006), *humanimal [a project for future children]* (Kelsey Street Press, 2009), *Schizophrene* (Nightboat, 2011), and *Ban en Banlieue* (Nightboat, 2015). Kapil has performed and under-performed internationally, most recently as part of the Serpentine's *Back To Earth* curation. She has recently returned to the UK after many years in the United States, where she taught across and beneath genres at Naropa University and Goddard College.

HOW TO WASH A HEART
PAVILION POETRY | £9.99 | PBS PRICE £7.50

This is a book which must be considered as a whole object. The title gushes into the first line and from there we are compelled through a series of... what word should I use... perhaps "scenes"? Yet this description only gives us half the picture. Partly this book feels brilliantly relentless, perhaps because of its connections to performance, and yet, formally, the decision to end-stop most lines, and have staccato short phrases run down the left-hand margin means that each line must be considered on its own. The reader immediately becomes aware of the multiple potential meanings inherent in each phrase, and is challenged to make their own connections as well. The tension of this construction, of the propensity of the verse together with contracted phrases, means that the poems are given a luminous three-dimensionality; rooms of possible meaning and interpretation are built for the reader to wander around in. Early on we get:

> To my left is a turquoise door and to my right a butcher's
> Table.
> Above you is a heart
> Beating in the snow.

The sense of direction becomes confused (the snow is above) and the capitalisation of each line, which might at first seem archaic, gives each line the force of a new statement, both joined by enjambement to its predecessor but also starting afresh. The multiplicity of potential meanings is not confusing though, nor deliberately exclusionary; Kapil's words sit brilliantly between the intellectual and the bodily.

The eponymous phrase of this book returns again and again, to be held up to the light in different ways. Violence, exile, love and the world of literature drip out in the answers to the opening question.

At the end of the collection we get an essay on its performative origins, yet this is a work that could only exist in this object of the book; a phrase like "how thyme migrates" draws its power from the visual rather than the aural.

SELECTOR'S COMMENT | ANDREW MCMILLAN

BHANU KAPIL

The entire book arrived all at once one day, as if it was being dictated by a very clear voice. It was distracting to be doing domestic things, or work outside of my home, when all I wanted to do was to get down what this voice was saying. Sometimes it was the voice of a guest and sometimes it was the voice of a host. After writing most of the first draft, I moved to the UK after twenty-one (or twenty-nine) years in the US. In Cambridge, I evolved a closing essay, *Notes on the Title*, trying to think about the performance at the ICA that inspired the title of this collection. It is unlikely I will ever write a book of poetry again. How did you feel when you read the last line of the book? Have you ever been welcomed into a space only to experience, once you've entered it, the aversion of its occupants? I was thinking about a country but I was also thinking about a university. Family memories of orchards and war mixed together, in what I wrote, with the Colorado morning, and the strange English night (which seemed to slam down, like a lid, at 3pm every afternoon.) The book's line breaks function, perhaps, in the way that the prose-poem did, when I first left the UK. I was following the sound of the voice, the phatic communion that presents itself as cordial, chatty. I remember something my father said when I was a child: "They smile behind their teeth." Perhaps it's obvious who he was speaking about, and perhaps it's not. Yes, I wanted to put that smile in my book. What does that smile conceal and oblate? Answering the question what inspired your book? I am no longer sure if I am writing in English, or thinking of English, or translating to an English of another kind, from another language, which I cannot speak. Perhaps what I'd like, most of all, is to keep asking questions about the relationship of poetry to conditions that are, in some sense, unsurvivable. This is an idea that came in response to Patrick Staff's *On Venus*, curated by Claude Adjil at the Serpentine. With a pencil, I wrote: "You can't survive here." Perhaps *How To Wash A Heart* will be something I read from, but really, even more than that, I would like to be in community with others, to keep sharing stories of belonging, unbelonging, hospitality and care.

BHANU RECOMMENDS

Mg Roberts, *Anemal Uter Meck* (Black Radish); Metta Sáma, *Swing at your own risk* (Kelsey Street Press); Melissa Buzzeo, *The Devastation* (Nightboat Books); M. NourbeSe Philip, *Zong!* (Wesleyan Poetry); Eunsong Kim, *Gospel of Regicide* (Noemi Press); Lucas de Lima, *Wet Land* (Action Books); Kim Eon Hee, *Have You Been Feeling Blue These Days?*, trans. Sung Gi Kim and Eunsong Kim (Noemi Press); Jennifer Tamayo, *Poems Are The Only Real Bodies* (Bloof Books); Mina Gorji, *Art of Escape* (Carcanet); Nisha Ramayya, *States of the Body Produced by Love* (Ignota Books); Jay Bernard, *Surge* (Chatto); Caspar Heinemann, *Novelty Theory* (The 87 Press) and Sandeep Parmar's as-yet-unpublished next book of poems.

HOW TO WASH A HEART

How to wash a heart:
Remove it.
Animal or ice?
The curator's question reveals
Their power style.
If power implies relationship,
Then here we are
At the part where even if something
Goes wrong,
That's exactly how it's meant to be.
Your job is to understand
What the feedback is.
It's such a pleasure to spend time
Outside the house.
There's nowhere to go with this
Except begin:
To plunge my forearms
Into the red ice
That is already melting
In the box.

The art of crisis
Is that you no longer
Think of home
As a place for social respite.
Instead, it's a ledge
Above a narrow canyon.
This is where you shit
And sleep, dreaming one night
Of jellyfish
In an aquarium
In Berlin, a factor
Of your European
Stay.
Beneath your clothes, you wear
A corset
Of bones, oil and
Cabbage leaves:
A sticky paste.
This causes shame
When it's time
To disrobe
In the facility.

Image: Alonso Parra

NATALIE DIAZ

Natalie Diaz is from Fort Mojave in Needles, California, on the Colorado River. She is Mojave and enrolled in the Gila River Indian Tribe. Her first poetry collection *When My Brother Was an Aztec* won an American Book Award. She is a 2018 MacArthur Fellow, a Lannan Literary Fellow and Native Arts Council Foundation Artist Fellow. She was awarded the Holmes National Poetry Prize. She is a member of the Board of Trustees for the United States Artists. Diaz is Maxine and Jonathan Marshall Chair in Modern and Contemporary Poetry and directs the Center for Imagination in the Borderlands at Arizona State University.

POSTCOLONIAL LOVE POEM
FABER | £10.99 | PBS PRICE £8.25

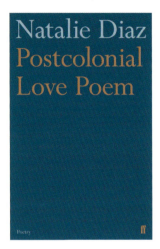

Natalie Diaz's *Postcolonial Love Poem* shares echoes with other American poets of late, many of whom have found their way to UK readers, especially those invested in social justice and violence against non-white Americans like Claudia Rankine, Layli Long Soldier and Danez Smith. Police brutality, historical violence against Native peoples, environmental destruction and the unravelling of languages under the dominance of English, occupy Diaz's book.

> The things I know aren't easy:
> I'm the only Native American
> on the 8th floor of this hotel or any,
> looking out any window
> of a turn-of-the-century building
> in Manhattan.
>
> Manhattan is a Lenape word.
> Even a watch must be wound.
> How can a century or a heart turn
> if nobody asks, *Where have all
> the Natives gone?*

SELECTOR'S COMMENT

Postcolonialism is mostly associated with countries outside the US – old colonial powers of Europe and the legacies of empire in Asia and Africa. But, as Diaz's book reminds readers, the US was a colonial project founded like most empires on genocide and enslavement of indigenous people. That the US has repurposed their postcolonial state into neo-colonialism is also not lost on Diaz: "We know how to speak to our conquerors, don't we?"

The extraordinary long poem 'The First Water Is the Body' conjures intention from language and slices skilfully through its powers with full authority. Lines like "I mean river as a verb. A happening. It is moving within me right now", raise the troubling problem of the oppressor's language as an act rather than a belonging. Mojave language, in particular, features here as an embodiment of resistance. To read Diaz's work is to see America anew and with the complexity it warrants, one imbued with silences and a colonial legacy that is so disgracefully overlooked in its own mythologising of a new and free world.

Sadly this publication has been delayed until September but PBS Members will receive their copies, as soon as possible, later in the Summer.

SANDEEP PARMAR

NATALIE DIAZ

This book is an inquiry into what it means to be a poet and how my relationship with language on the page can help me to live off of and beyond the page. What does it mean to practice poetry, to recognise it as a method for the ways I imagine and enact my beloveds and strangers alike, my Native language and English language, my autonomous and love-possible self within a terrible nation? The poetical imagination has taught me that desire is made equally of sorrow and pleasure, as am I. What does it mean for a person with a body like mine – a body with wounds both earned and inherited, both self- and empire-inflicted – to desire something more than my country has designed for me?

These poems indulge in desire as imagination – a condition in which desire becomes more than a want at the end of my hands, where desire becomes the hand itself, what it might yet touch or invite of touching. I found these poems in the chasms between what is and what is yet to be – which is not a place of lack or dearth, but instead a place where I pleasure in the unknown of what or who I might become, which is the unknown of what and who we once were.

These poems are my intention to exist in America not against or because of this nation but as something beyond it, because life was given to me, as my own, as an energy in relationship with the earth. I am asking: Can I return to the conditions that our Creators first made for us: a land and a river held inside a body of abundance. Can I act less like a descendant of the past and more like an ancestor of the future? I am at once what I have been and what I have yet to be – isn't this also the nature of language?

NATALIE RECOMMENDS

Etel Adnan, *Of Cities & Women* (Letters to Fawwaz); Dionne Brand, *Ossuaries* (McClelland & Stewart); Eduardo C. Corral, *Guillotine* (Graywolf Press); Zoe Leonard and Dolores Dorantes, *El Río / The River: A Collaboration* (Gato Negro Ediciones); Nathalie Handal, *Life In A Country Album* (University of Pittsburgh Press); Dunya Mikhail, trans. Elizabeth Winslow, *The War Works Hard* (New Directions); Sara Uribe, trans. John Pluecker, *Antígona González* (Les Figues Press).

I've been taught bloodstones can cure a snakebite,
can stop the bleeding—most people forgot this
when the war ended. The war ended
depending on which war you mean: those we started,
before those, millennia ago and onward,
those which started me, which I lost and won—
these ever-blooming wounds.
I was built by wage. So I wage love and worse—
always another campaign to march across
a desert night for the cannon flash of your pale skin
settling in a silver lagoon of smoke at your breast.
I dismount my dark horse, bend to you there, deliver you
the hard pull of all my thirsts—
I learned *Drink* in a country of drought.
We pleasure to hurt, leave marks
the size of stones—each a cabochon polished
by our mouths. I, your lapidary, your lapidary wheel
turning—green mottled red—
the jaspers of our desires.
There are wildflowers in my desert
which take up to twenty years to bloom.
The seeds sleep like geodes beneath hot feldspar sand
until a flash flood bolts the arroyo, lifting them
in its copper current, opens them with memory—
they remember what their god whispered
into their ribs: *Wake up and ache for your life.*
Where your hands have been are diamonds
on my shoulders, down my back, thighs—
I am your culebra.
I am in the dirt for you.
Your hips are quartz-light and dangerous,
two rose-horned rams ascending a soft desert wash
before the November sky untethers a hundred-year flood—
the desert returned suddenly to its ancient sea.
Arise the wild heliotrope, scorpion weed,
blue phacelia which hold purple the way a throat can hold
the shape of any great hand—
Great hands is what she called mine.
The rain will eventually come, or not.
Until then, we touch our bodies like wounds—
the war never ended and somehow begins again.

THE CURE FOR MELANCHOLY IS TO TAKE THE HORN

Powdered unicorn horn was once thought to cure melancholy.

What carries the hurt is never the wound
    but the red garden sewn by the horn
as it left—and she left. I am rosing,
    blossoming absence—a brilliant alarum.

Brodsky said, *Darkness restores what light cannot*
    repair. You thrilled me—torn to the comb.
I want everything—the ebon bull and the moon.
    I come and again for the honeyed horn.

Queen Elizabeth traded a castle for a single horn.
    I serve the kingdom of my hands—
an army of touch marching the alcázar of your thighs
    blaring and bright as any war horn.

I arrive at you—half bestia, half feast.
    Night after night we harvest the luxed Bosque
de Caderas, reap the darkful fruit mulling our mouths,
    separate sweet from thorn.

My lanternist. Your hands wick at the bronzed
    lamp of my breast. Strike me to spark—
tremble me to awe. Into your lap
    let me lay my heavy horns.

I fulfilled the prophecy of your throat, loosed in you
    the fabulous wing of my mouth. Red holy-red
ghost. Left my body and spoke to God, came back
    seraphimed—copper feathered and horned.

Our bodies are nothing if not places to be had by,
    as in, *God, she had me by the throat,*
by the hip bone, by the moon. God,
    she hurt me with my own horns.

NATALIE DIAZ

Image: Etienne Gilfillan

ELLA FREARS

Ella Frears is a poet and visual artist based in London. Her poems have appeared in *The London Review of Books, Poetry London, Ambit,* and *The Rialto* among others. She was a finalist for the Arts Foundation Fellowship in Poetry, is a trustee and editor for *Magma* poetry magazine and has completed residencies for the National Trust, Tate Britain, K6 Gallery and Royal Holloway University. Her poems about the St Ives Modernists are currently on show at Tate St Ives. Ella's poem 'Fucking in Cornwall' was commended in this year's National Poetry Competition.

SHINE, DARLING
OFFORD ROAD BOOKS | £10.00 | PBS PRICE £7.50

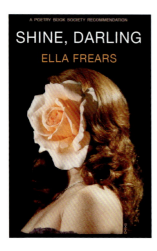

Ella Frears' debut collection *Shine, Darling* might remind readers of recent collections that take up the familiar (to some) subjects of the adolescent female body and sexuality. Class, Englishness and region (Cornwall especially), shame, violence, cruelty, and deep sardonic humour at times make one wish to place Frears in a pantheon with poets like Rachael Allen, Sophie Collins, Amy Key, and AK Blakemore. But there's something very unique about this poet's voice, emerging as others do from a social and political moment that intersects with the vulnerability and fragility of girls. And even though the work is at times humorous it is also more often deeply unsettling – unwilling, perhaps, to oversimplify innocence through a complex and ambivalent lyricism. Buoyed up by precise and unadorned language, Frears' speakers slip into and out of power with unnerving speed.

In 'The Film', two young women embark on an art project that seems harmless, maybe even a bit noble, as part of a wider commentary on male violence.

> The sun was shining as we
> ambled around campus
> stopping boys and men
> and asking them to hit me
> across the face.

Most of the men are of course mortified and comply with tenderness – except for one. The crisis of the poem – which an explanation would spoil – amounts to an uneasy lesson about control, play, intimacy and trust.

Elsewhere, the grotesquerie of girlhood brings blushes to anyone who remembers what it is like to age and be suddenly visible in a hostile world of temptations and predators. A previously published selection included here, 'Passivity, Electricity, Acclivity', returns us to the sparse and sometimes pitiless narrative of monstrous women and the violence we do to each other. Frears is abundantly intelligent and the quality of her language forces us to take responsibility for inaction as much as action.

SANDEEP PARMAR

ELLA FREARS

While reading a *New Yorker* article last year about the strange scandal surrounding a deceitful novelist, I was struck, not by the big lies he told, but by an account of a conference call that two former colleagues remembered having with him. Throughout the call the novelist kept shouting at a dog – "No! Get Down!" After he hung up, the colleagues looked at each other – "there's no dog, right?" "No."

I'm interested in the multiple selves we create on and off the page – in how these selves rub up against or disrupt one another. The poems in my book are open – plainly written and often anecdotal or confessional. At the heart of *Shine, Darling* is a lyric essay – interwoven narratives that circle around a very real near-abduction experience. Small moments of intimacy interlock with stories about spies, death, a stalker. I wanted to write a long-form poem the length and weight of a short story, with the suspense of a novel. A while back, I went to see Deborah Levy give a talk. She discussed her love of detective fiction and (sorry Deborah, if I've misremembered) said something along the lines of – I want to write one where it's the protagonist's sense of self that's been murdered. I love this idea.

In her essay on the "Metaphysical I", Dorothea Lasky writes that "the best gift that a poet can give his or her 'I' is to allow it to be its own cool animal." I want the reader to feel like my lyric "I" is talking to them. I want them to trust my "I", she has my name, she's so like me. But I also want the poems to have an atmosphere – a feeling you can't quite place until at some point you close the book and think... wait, there's no dog, right?

ELLA RECOMMENDS

Currently I'm enjoying Sharon Olds, CAConrad, Kim Hyesoon, Brenda Shaughnessy, Michael Earl Craig, Terrance Hayes, Lisa Kelly, Franny Choi, Holly Pester and Fran Lock. You should also read anything by Anne Carson – my favourite is *The Beauty of the Husband*; *Bunny*, Selima Hill (Bloodaxe); *Tender Taxes*, Jo Shapcott (Faber); *Dear Big Gods*, Mona Arshi (Pavilion Poetry); *Poems 1962-2012*, Louise Glück (FSG); *Dunce*, Mary Ruefle and her essays on poetry (Wave); *Poems New and Collected*, Wisława Szymborska (Roundhouse).

How will we go on after, I thought...

I ASKED HIM TO CHECK THE ROOF, THEN TOOK THE LADDER AWAY

All night I enjoyed the lie: *not feeling well, upstairs in bed but
sends his love.*

I could feel his frustration through the ceiling; so strongly
that it was as though my chest were the roof and he was
trapped
inside. *How will we go on after*, I thought, *how will I end this?*

He hadn't called for help. Maybe he'd worked out a way down
but I didn't think so. The dinner party was wonderful.
As the guests left I looked up and realised that there was no
moon.

Shine, darling. I whispered. And from behind the chimney
rose his little head.

Image: Brid O'Donovan

SEÁN HEWITT

Seán Hewitt is a research fellow at University College Cork and a book critic for *The Irish Times*. His pamphlet *Lantern* (Offord Road Books) was the Poetry Book Society Summer Pamphlet Choice in 2019, and won an Eric Gregory Award. He won the Resurgence Prize (now the Ginkgo Prize) in 2017, and a Northern Writers' Award in 2016. *Tongues of Fire* is his first collection.

TONGUES OF FIRE
CAPE | £10.00 | PBS PRICE £7.50

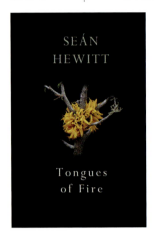

Seán Hewitt's *Tongues of Fire* largely eschews direct treatment of the torments of global politics or social justice, favouring instead a transcendent almost nostalgic quietude of recollection. Carefully crafted lines, scenes of nature imbued with sometimes spiritual, sometimes human, matters focus the reader's eye on the effulgence of a moment, that lyric premise which is still unshakably central to poetry. If the tongues of fire, sent in biblical myth to the apostles as an embodiment of the holy spirit, are here a form of overlying witness, then Hewitt's poems spread a muted gospel tied to the landscape and human intimacies. Bold in their exploration of queerness, lust, and sex, the juxtaposition of this with a conventionally Romantic foraging for symbols is acutely perceived and moving at times.

A wish to communicate through visits and visitations might be one way to consider this book's dual urge towards silence and speech. There are visits to woods, hospitals, friends, family, populated by vibrant linguistically unusual flora and equally non-descript or anonymous people. The effects of nature and memory on the body are the most vivid of all.

> All of a sudden it stops me –
> acrid and sour-white, wafting
> in sheets as the pollen catches the sun
>
> then billows upwards –
> the same smell, loosing now
> in drifts through the hot streets

The scent of Callery pear, evidently similar to bodily odours, mingles with the embodied memory of sex or, likely, masturbation. A kind of ecstatic and simultaneous mingling of senses – past, present, even future – suddenly erupts here over five short and controlled tercets.

Hewitt's work is a balm for anyone who craves formalism and lyric address. Dashes, the carefully split word, a judicious parenthesis, and a whispering over bodies, trees, etc. all this combines like an incantation, prayer, a kind of gospel of the self.

SANDEEP PARMAR

SEÁN HEWITT

On the cover of the collection is an image of a rust fungus, *gymnosporangium clavariiforme*, or "Tongues of Fire". It can't go unnoticed that these are tongues, speaking from the branch, something sacred becoming physical, something spiritual pushing out into the matter of the world, something unspoken being given voice.

That fungus is emblematic of many of the poems in *Tongues of Fire*. Over time, I realised a lot of my poems were working away at a boundary where nature, the body, and something beyond the body, meld and interact, speaking to each other or *of* each other. The collection, I think, has two underlying questions: Where does physical matter start and end? And where, too, does our search for meaning start, and where should it end?

I have two poetic fascinations: a poetry of the body, which is an inheritance from queer writers, and a poetry of the natural world seen slant. In *Tongues of Fire*, I hope, these two things come together, and are rarely distinct.

The book is in four parts. The fourth section was written last. My father died on the day I signed the contract for *Tongues of Fire*, and those final poems deal with all the world-tilting confusion of losing a parent, and try to map the strangeness of the world as it appeared to me in those months. They are, in a sense, pre-elegies; they are also poems that I wish I never had the occasion to write.

But I hope that readers might find here the consolation of commonality. They might see an altered perspective; or might recognise, in the words of the final poem, "love's fragility, its immanence // in the body, the proximity it takes / to material form."

SEÁN RECOMMENDS

Carl Phillips, *Quiver of Arrows: Selected Poems, 1986-2006* (FSG); David Harsent, *Loss* (Faber); Helen Tookey, *City of Departures* (Carcanet); Andrew McMillan, *playtime* (Cape); Jos Charles, *Feeld* (Milkweed); Tua Forsström, *One Evening in October I Rowed Out on the Lake*, trans. David McDuff (Bloodaxe); Medbh McGuckian, *Marine Cloud Brightening* (Gallery); Richie Hofmann, *Second Empire* (Alice James) and Mina Gorji, *Art of Escape* (Carcanet).

...something akin to happiness

Image: Martin Stephens

ST JOHN'S WORT

Named for a man who carries his own head
on a platter, for a day when the sun bears
its light over the land so slowly, so measuredly,
that the night crouches back and waits. A token
of love, of patience, of the will to lift the mind
outside oneself, and let it rest. Let it heal. Alone,
I remembered this little herb, the yellow spikes
of the flower, frill of stamen, as something akin
to happiness – its bright stars, its tiny play
at hope, its way of lifting through the grass –
and I brought it to you, a light to illumine
the dark caves of your eyes. At the door
of the ward, being searched, the nurse
took from me my gathering of flowers.
I found you on the bed, staring, still in shock.
Bringing no gift, I took your head
in my empty hands like a world and held it.

Image: Nancy Adajania-Utrecht

RANJIT HOSKOTE

Ranjit Hoskote is a poet, cultural theorist and curator. He is the author of six collections of poetry, including *Vanishing Acts: New & Selected Poems 1985-2005* (Penguin, 2006) and *Central Time* (Penguin / Viking, 2014). He has translated the 14th-century Kashmiri mystic Lal Ded's poetry as *I, Lalla: The Poems of Lal Ded* (Penguin Classics, 2011). He is the editor of *Dom Moraes: Selected Poems* (Penguin Modern Classics, 2012). Hoskote was curator of India's first-ever national pavilion at the Venice Biennale (2011) and co-curated the 7th Gwangju Biennale (2008). He is Poetry Editor for *DOMUS India*, and lives in Bombay.

THE ATLAS OF LOST BELIEFS
ARC | £11.99 | PBS PRICE £9.00

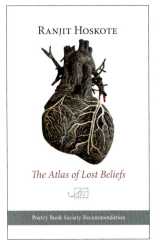

RANJIT HOSKOTE

The Atlas of Lost Beliefs

Poetry Book Society Recommendation

The trouble with trying to tell you about a book like this is that any words will fall flat when attempting to pay tribute to the way this language crackles and fizzes, the surrealism tinged with violence, the echoes of Ashbery or Selima Hill put into a global context and mapped onto the histories of trades and slavery.

An early poem like 'The Map Seller' exemplifies this excitement; "The roof's dripping with pigeons and I've just escaped / the worst of the sun" begin the opening couple of lines. That unexpected arrival of pigeon after "dripping" immediately puts the poem on an odd kilter.

Later in the same poem, though, we get the other part of Hoskote's mission, when we are given the "flaking jigsaw atlas"; this is a world breaking apart, where language is at an angle, where the signifier and the signified no longer match up, where, as in a later poem, a "reckless dancer" is "Cossack-kicking on a crumbling reef".

To purely focus on the brilliance of the language here would be a mistake, though; these poems are crossing oceans, sometimes literally, often metaphorically (water returns again and again throughout the collection) in order to reckon with history. Perhaps in the sea-shanty rhythms of 'Cargo and Ballast', or the "wide fan-spread hood of this coiled sea-cobra we're sailing" which is at once a specific vessel but also the collective propulsion of history and its violences.

"Countries are working hypotheses that sometimes fail" states one poem, a poem in which, not for the first time, creepers appear; history again, seeping into the present. This is a vital collection examining the ways in which we receive history and the ways we build contemporary myths in order to look back over our shoulders.

The Poet's Life:

He married birdsong.
He sailed to the black island.
He survived gunshots.
He wore a sweatshirt under his linen jacket.
He talked to parrots in Greek.

ANDREW McMILLAN

RANJIT HOSKOTE

I was born and grew up by the sea, in Bombay and Goa on India's west coast. *The Atlas of Lost Beliefs* is animated by the sea, its histories of migration, the way it acts as a crucible for new languages, new identities. My starting points for this book come from the pluriverse I inhabit as a writer and reader across languages, cultures, and periods. Among these are Melville's *Moby-Dick* and Saint-John Perse's book-length poem, *Anabase*, translated by TS Eliot in 1930 as *Anabasis*, as well as the Martiniquais philosopher Édouard Glissant's *Poetics of Relation*, and René Char's *La parole en archipel*. I've also been nourished by sources outside poetry, by pre- and non-Columbian maps such as those of al-Idrisi, Piri Reis, and Zheng He, cartographers and navigators in whose work I have long been immersed. Another point of departure for me is the *muraqqa*, the album prized by the Safavid, Mughal and Ottoman visual cultures. It was part portfolio, part scrapbook, part journal, binding together original paintings, prints, calligraphic annotation, and text. In 'Cargo and Ballast', different voices, extracts from judicial documents, maritime records, the phantom of a Turner painting, and pop-cultural references, all come together into a *muraqqa* that mourns the victims of the slave trade: "If you're healthy, the plantation. / If you're sick, the cutlass or the sharks. / You're cargo. / You could so easily / be ballast." *The Atlas of Lost Beliefs* opens up to accommodate silences and erasures, the word visible yet cancelled, voiced yet unvoiced, perhaps to be rendered *sotto voce*. Collage, montage, the cut-up, looping, antiphony, all come into play as formative and integral devices in the making of these poems. I'm preoccupied with questions of temporality: duration, simultaneity, counterpoint. I've turned back, during the writing of this book, to the music of Steve Reich, Terry Riley and Brian Eno, and to the maverick William S. Burroughs, who pioneered cut-up and fold-in techniques with Brion Gysin. As Burroughs says in *The Job* (1969), "you can do all sorts of things on tape recorders which can't be done anywhere else – effects of simultaneity, echoes, speed-ups, slow-downs, playing three tracks at once... There are all sorts of things you can do on a tape recorder that cannot possibly be indicated on a printed page." *The Atlas of Lost Beliefs* tries, modestly, to explore these possibilities.

RANJIT RECOMMENDS

Ruth Padel, *Beethoven Variations* (Chatto); Michael Kelleher, *Visible Instruments* (CHAX); James Byrne, *Everything Broken Up Dances* (Tupelo); Ishion Hutchinson, *House of Lords and Commons* (Faber); Sandeep Parmar, *The Marble Orchard* (Shearsman); Hope Mirrlees, *Collected Poems* (Carcanet); Valzhyna Mort, *Collected Body* (Copper Canyon Press); Nikola Madzirov, *Remnants of Another Age* (Boa Editions); Alvin Pang, *When the Barbarians Arrive* (Arc); Yves Bonnefoy, *The Present Hour,* trans. Beverley Bie Brahic (Seagull) and Osip Mandelstam, *The Moscow and Voronezh Notebooks*, trans. Richard and Elizabeth McKane (Bloodaxe).

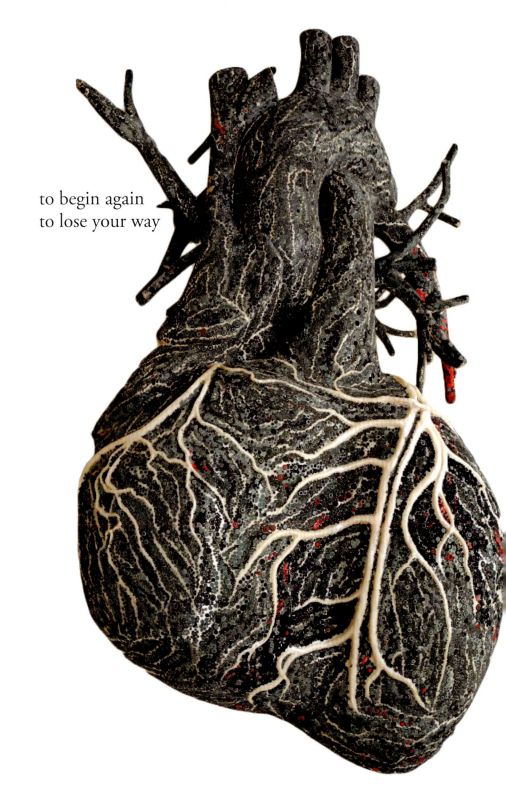
to begin again
to lose your way

THE HEART FIXES ON NOTHING

Zafar

The heart fixes on nothing in this wasted province.
Whoever made anything of a kingdom of shadows?

Go find another home, my smothered hopes.
This stained heart has no roof to offer you.

I prayed for long life and got four days:
two were spent in desire, two in waiting.

Gardener, don't rip these thorns from the garden:
they were raised with the roses by a gentle spring.

The nightingale doesn't blame the gardener or the hunter:
Fate had decided spring would be its cage.

Fate's real dupe: that would be you, Zafar, your body denied
two yards of spaded earth in the Loved One's country.

A translation of the Mughal emperor and poet Bahadur Shah Zafar's ghazal,
'Lagta nahi hai dil mera'.

GRACE NICHOLS

Born in Guyana, Grace Nichols has lived in Britain since 1977. Her first collection, *I is a Long Memoried Woman* (1983) won the Commonwealth Poetry Prize. Her later poetry collections, published by Virago, include *The Fat Black Woman's Poems* (1984), *Lazy Thoughts of a Lazy Woman* (1989), *Sunris* (1996), winner of the Guyana Prize, and *Startling the Flying Fish* (2006), along with several poetry books for younger readers, including *Come on into My Tropical Garden* (1988), *Give Yourself a Hug* (1994), *Everybody Got a Gift* (2005) and *Cosmic Disco* (2013). She has published three books with Bloodaxe, *Picasso, I Want My Face Back* (2009), *I Have Crossed an Ocean: Selected Poems* (2010), and *The Insomnia Poems* (2017). She lives in Sussex with the poet John Agard and their family.

PASSPORT TO HERE AND THERE
BLOODAXE | £9.95 | PBS PRICE £7.47

This collection is held together by a sense of returning, and a desire to save things from erasure. Through the different poetic forms and meditations, through the photographs, and through the prose introduction to the book, we get a sense of a poet enacting both redemption and leaving. These poems, like the book itself, are split between England and Guyana, between childhood memories and adult experience, between observation of the now and excavation of history. As with all of Nichols' work, this collection shows how poetry can translate the world, not only for the reader, but for the poet themselves; one gets the sense that these poems are bridges, between the poet and her past, between nations, but also between other poets and Nichols' own work. A memorable poem, 'Greensleeves' might be a rewriting of Heaney's third section of 'Clearances', whilst elsewhere Wilfred Owen is reconsidered and, towards the end of the book, there is a moving elegy for Derek Walcott.

One of Nichols' great gifts is to make poems which don't merely describe something (though if that's your bag then she can do it as well as anyone, the "jigsaw puzzle of drought" for example, or the brilliant description of waves which turns up in 'Nuptial on Brighton Beach'). Rather, this is work which feels as though it has a constant propulsion, pulling the poet (and therefore the reader) with it. This is not a static collection, it is not weighed down despite its history and despite its intelligence; it is a collection which floats free and is able to cross continents on behalf of its readers.

The sonnet 'reunion' is perhaps a stand-out poem from this expansive collection: as the poet steps out into the "equatorial night", they are welcomed by the "back-home rooted ones", as though they were "returning astronauts" being welcomed "in their arms of gravity".

> And even if no one had come to meet me
> as I stepped out into the equatorial night
> (baggage-burdened yet unbelievably light)
> I would have probably grabbed and planted
> a kiss on somebody – one of those homely
> faces craning towards me like dark
> expectant sunflowers in the waiting crowd –

Available to pre-order; publication is postponed until July.
ANDREW McMILLAN

APPLE AND MANGO

When last home, trying to recover
some of the bright light of small-girl days,
my sister threw me the sudden gift
of a Buxton Spice mango.

I remember how I peeled and sliced
that plump orb of sunshine,
adding a sprinkling of salt,
the way I liked it as a child.

I remember how she raised her eyes
when I said I'd leave back for *afters*, a slice –
Girl, you can't finish one mango?

How could I have admitted
that I had to save back space
for the fruits of my other back-home –

This rain and winter-driven Blighty
where summery strawberry
and apple and my daughters all grow.

THE TRANSLATORS

Loretta Collins Klobah is the author of two poetry collections. *The Twelve Foot Neon Woman* (Peepal Tree Press, 2011) received the OCM Bocas Prize for Caribbean poetry and was short-listed for the Forward's Felix Dennis Prize. She has received many awards, including the Pushcart Prize, the Earl Lyons Award from The Academy of American Poets, and the Pam Wallace Award for an Aspiring Woman Writer. Her poems have been widely published in journals and anthologies. She lives in San Juan, Puerto Rico, where she is Professor of Caribbean Literature and Creative Writing at The University of Puerto Rico.

Maria Grau Perejoan, holds a doctoral degree in Cultural Studies with an emphasis on Caribbean Literature and Literary Translation from the University of Barcelona, and an MPhil in Cultural Studies from the University of the West Indies, Trinidad and Tobago. She was visiting lecturer at the UWI, St Augustine Campus for three academic years, she then moved on to lecture courses in Translation and Caribbean Literature at the University of Barcelona, and since 2020 she is a Lecturer at the Department of Spanish, Modern and Classical Languages at the University of the Balearic Islands.

THE SEA NEEDS NO ORNAMENT
LORETTA COLLINS KLOBAH AND MARIA GRAU PEREJOAN
PEEPAL TREE PRESS | £14.99 | PBS PRICE £11.25

Thirty-three poets from the English and Spanish-speaking Caribbean in this book give us some of the most passionate, and insightful writing around, in any language, but as I look at translated voices here, I am both moved and transformed by the ways they seem to address the devastation of our current moment. For example, Karol Starocean from Santo Domingo, shows "how the emergency sirens don't stop blinking... there are no fish or fishermen" because a hurricane "wishes to salute us down to the bone." While Thais Espaillat, also from Santo Domingo, brings a more humorous perspective, she also gives us a nuanced lyric strangeness. Extraterrestrials, the poet says, "don't talk to us because we are boring"

Or maybe they know so much that they don't even talk anymore...
and they show up in some photos...
with slobber that awakens a distant volcano.
I am sure that extraterrestrials don't write poetry...
They don't cook on television

A few pages later, Mara Pastor from Puerto Rico, also begins on a humorous note, but quickly becomes political, addressing a deserted nation:

If everything continues like this,
If everyone leaves now
...the island will be taken over
By iguanas
And lion fish.
They will make a bust of me.
It will be easy to be the national poet
among bush-chicken iguanas.

And meanwhile, Jamila Medina Ríos from Holguin, gives this solitude a personal urgency: "When they take me to the insane asylum, handcuffed, in anguish, I will not transmute myself into fish or a fresh slice of cucumber; I'm going to sit in a corner and think about how to become the nothing of cork, a mirage, steam over tea". These and other Spanish-speaking poets are presented in this book together with such wonderful English-language Caribbean poets as Malika Booker, Shara McCallum, and Safiya Sinclair. The result is a first-rate conversation between poetics, a marvel.

ILYA KAMINSKY

DANGEROUS THINGS

This is the island.
It is small and vulnerable,
it is a woman, calling. You love her
until you are a part of her
and then, just like that,
you make her less than she was
before – the space
that you take up
is a space where she cannot exist.
It is
something in her history
that does this,
don't mind
her name. The island
is a woman, therefore
dangerous things live below,
beautiful things, also – which can be the most dangerous.
True, we will never be
beyond our histories.
And so I am the island.
And so this is a warning.

ALYCIA PIRMOHAMED

Alycia Pirmohamed is the author of the pamphlets *Faces That Fled the Wind* (selected by Camille Rankine for the 2018 BOAAT Press Chapbook Prize) and *Hinge* (ignitionpress). Her awards include the Gulf Coast Poetry Prize, the CBC Poetry Prize, the Sawti Poetry Prize in English, the 92Y Discovery Poetry Contest, and the Ploughshares' Emerging Writer's Contest in Poetry. Her work has recently appeared, or is forthcoming, in *The Paris Review Daily, Guernica Magazine, Poetry London Magazine*, and others. Alycia received her MFA from the University of Oregon, and she is currently a PhD student at the University of Edinburgh.

HINGE BY ALYCIA PIRMOHAMED
IGNITION PRESS | £5.00 |

Hinge is a shimmering and moving pamphlet of lyric poems which dwells exquisitely on the intricacies of being "someone who stepped into this world already in halves", as a migrant living in a world of nation-states where borders sharply delineate where one's "homeland" officially begins and ends. This does not easily map onto one's sense of belonging, however, as the speaker in 'Homeward' observes:

In the heart of every migrant, there is a windrose pointing hor and while the needles within your own cells

flicker back and forth, your father is steadfast in direction: homeward, a course you have only ever imagined, a flight path

These poems often cover vast swathes of ground while remaining deeply intimate in their ability to probe intertwined relationships with one's family, country of origin and chosen homeland. Pirmohamed tenderly explores her cultural heritages that are encoded in Arabic, Gujarati and English, as well as in the landscapes of Jasper, Alberta:

> I had longed to find the hidden trail that led to the valley of roses.
>
> From the elk, I am expecting a lesson, as if Allah has approached me in the shape of a compass built from antler and vine.
> Their muscles tense. One rises into a gallop, widening the field.
>
> Its legs seize with strength and I remain in the space left behind:
> the sudden nakedness of a northern forest. I am unable to follow—
> the elk, in their way, have mastered living by mastering letting go.
>
> – Elegy with Two Elks and a Compass

Religion, philosophy and personal memories often meld into one another in these tensile and crystalline poems, as Pirmohamed's speakers resist clarity or resolution, opting instead for the nuances and complex ambiguities of what it means to live (and remember) across multiple geographies and histories. This is a pamphlet to savour and relish.

Available to pre-order.

WHEN THE WOLVES APPEAR

When the wolves appear, I know I am dreaming.
Give me back my dark. They call out in Gujarati & no howling
could terrify me as much. The wolf-eyes, like eyes in family photographs,
follow me. I run & don't look back.
I am terrified of the land. At sea, my body is a vase
filled with ovate black stones. I sink
I sink I sink. Where have the wolves gone & where is the voice
that held the whorls of my fingers in its clay?
Is it fair to wish for them now? They don't belong in this version of a version
of India that wets my hair & deposits my skin onto the shore—
to get to the bone. To get to the language.
I want to say *yes* I want to become a stream of milk
& wash through the aquifers. To pick up dark stalks of sugar along the way.
I want to carry my dark with me. Stretch out legs of jasmine vine &
call out to the deep space between the stars. Every night I open my mouth.
Every night, my mouth is an orbiting, elliptical *no.*

ALYCIA PIRMOHAMED

WAYNE HOLLOWAY-SMITH was born in Wiltshire and lives in London. He co-edits the online journal *Poems in Which* and teaches at the University of Hertfordshire. His first collection, *Alarum* (Bloodaxe, 2017) won the PBS Wild Card Choice, was shortlisted for the Roehampton Poetry Prize, the Seamus Heaney Centre for Poetry Prize for First Full Collection, and longlisted for the Michael Murphy Memorial Prize. In 2018 he won the National Poetry Competition.

LOVE MINUS LOVE

one story goes a man on his lunch break was hit
   by a falling baby falling from a very high window
of a building the man was passing on his lunch break
the man saved the baby's life accidentally getting landed on
   the man saved that exact baby's life accidentally getting landed on
one exact year later   on his lunch break breaking
the slightly-more-grown-baby-falling-
from-the-same-window's fall accidentally
the man's name is   Joseph Figlock what is sad is
the realisation this baby
could literally mean anything
but doesn't
it does not
what I don't know is whether that baby
a toddler by now   has fallen a third time
whether he is falling still and at this moment crying out
where is Joseph Figlock I can't see him why isn't he here

WILD CARD CHOICE

LOVE MINUS LOVE
BLOODAXE | £10.99 | PBS PRICE £8.25

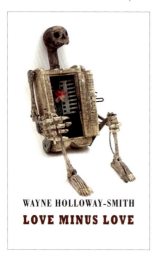

Let's get down to the
boiled beef of it let's get
down to the canned ham
the corned beef hash of it.

Such inventive, memorable and sardonic phrase making fills Wayne Holloway-Smith's second collection *Love Minus Love*. A startling and unconventional experiment rooted in childhood, place, masculinity and the environment, Holloway-Smith bridges seemingly disparate subjects to create a coherent and tender experience.

"Meanwhile the woman who will one day be your mother / is busy turning her belly into a butcher's shop." In a sequence of untitled poems, often appearing as protracted, imagistic meditations shifting from a son's relationship with his parents, to the illogical constructs of gender binaries, Holloway-Smith compels the reader into an alarming vision of consequences. The interplay between past and present, between platonic friendship and intimacy, and how the male body has been usurped to act as a nefarious emblem of strength and resilience, all align to challenge and subvert sociosymbolic preconceptions.

In the dream... his father was alive once more and was
talking to him in his usual way but the remarkable thing was
that he was nevertheless dead only did not know it.

The narratives move and dip in continuously surprising ways. From soliloquising with an imagined character named David, to recurring conversations with a deceased father, the work resists linearity, instead choosing to sweep and organise multiple conceits into grammarless blocks of poetic thought. The final notable motif, which reoccurs, is the way food and the body coalesce to speak to a juxtaposing emptiness.

what is sad is I wrote your name all over my jeans
keep the jeans keep the three-meat sandwich we ate
the rap song we made up together in a bedroom at
your house then mine with our parents getting
drunk downstairs and despising each other...

Available to pre-order; publication is postponed until July.

ANTHONY ANAXAGOROU

WAYNE HOLLOWAY-SMITH

In the early moments of her 'Conversation with Adrienne Rich', the poet Audre Lorde seems to suggest a world of non-verbal personal experiences for which there is yet no vocabulary, but which we can come close to expressing through poetry. This is the way poetry works for me, it's the reason it matters so much. It's also the reason that I'm hesitant to try to explain what my work's trying to do or its themes. I mean, if poetry provides me, as it does for us all, an opportunity to move past the limitations the English language places upon my experiences, then perhaps it's disingenuous to transpose how I have employed this expansive opportunity – back into the narrowness of common language-based explanation. I want, instead, to use the space I've been given to highlight some things to which my book and I are indebted.

First, the many examples of how emotional experience and internal landscapes might be expressed in this art-form we love. Some examples come from friends – Emily Berry, Raymond Antrobus, Helen Charman, Jack Underwood, Nuar Alsadir to mention a few. Also, the writers and thinkers whose work continues to have an enormous impact upon how I perceive and put into poetic vocabulary aspects of my world. Some of these voices appear in *Love Minus Love*, because this feels an honest and necessary way of representing their contribution to my understanding. There have been a number of significant relationships which have nurtured my confidence to continue writing, this includes the one with my editor Neil Astley, whose support for this book has been incredible. People who teach me daily that courage and love are practices into which I need to lean: my mother, my partner, my daughter. Lastly, people who have shown me their empathy by reading my work. I'm grateful for all of this. Thank you.

WAYNE RECOMMENDS

Rachael Allen, *Kingdomland* (Faber); Susannah Dickey, *Bloodthirsty for Marriage* (Bad Betty Press); CAConrad, *While Standing in Line for Death* (Wave Books); Bell Hooks, *All About Love: New Visions* (HarperCollins); Silvia Federici, *Caliban and the Witch* (Autonomedia); Franny Choi, *Soft Science* (Alice James Books); Kim Hyesoon, *Autobiography of Death* (New Directions Books); Morgan Parker, *Other People's Comfort Keeps Me Up At Night* (Switchback Books); Jacqueline Rose, *Mothers: An Essay on Love and Cruelty* (Faber) and Han Kang, *The White Book* (Portobello Books).

I WILD CARD CHOICE

SUMMER BOOK REVIEWS

LINDA ANDERSON: THE STATION BEFORE

"This is not a place to settle": it is a journey through memory and its many interruptions. "Tilted between past and present", a childhood in post-war Scotland and the death of a Father, Anderson surveys the tender remnants of life, "a pair of compasses, three erasers, hard as stones". Images recur with visionary clarity, lapwings, kittiwakes, photographs and the fraught art of seeing: "But what does seeing mean? / I was looking through a door, half-open". In these lyrical and liminal poems "arrival is a myth" and we can only ever reach *The Station Before*.

PAVILION POETRY | £9.99 | PBS PRICE £7.50

ADAM CROTHERS: THE CULTURE OF MY STUFF

Crothers' lyrical wordplay is a joy to read. Part of this joy is decoding his cryptic taste in metaphor: "Baby I'm bored on a train. Look, stranger: tunnel vision, lo-fi loupe, // creeping monocular leer. This moment's owed no monument so it's a leap // to be crafting one here". Crothers' subjects are too multifarious to be constrained by definition. All is driven onwards by an impeccable sense of rhythm.

CARCANET | £10.99 | PBS PRICE £8.25

THEOPHILUS KWEK: MOVING HOUSE

This prize-winning Chinese-Singaporean writer moves deftly across continents from Singapore to Oxford, past to present. Whether probing Einstein's black holes or witnessing an accident, Kwek has a keen eye for poetic rupture and moments of collision. With formal dexterity, he sifts through family history and world politics, from British colonial rule to refugee crises and a moving tribute to soldiers killed in peacetime training: "we /are   boys young men   and scared of dying".

CARCANET | £10.99 | PBS   PRICE   £8.25

DEBORAH LANDAU: SOFT TARGETS

Partly a work of protest poetry, partly an exploration of mortality, *Soft Targets* responds to the tragedies of mass shootings, neo-fascism and gun-fetishism. Landau paints the human body's grip on life as alarmingly precarious; we are the titular "soft targets". Wrestling with how to navigate such a violent world, and how one could possibly justify bringing a child into it, Landau's verse is not simply morbid, but brilliant and refreshingly uncompromising.

BLOODAXE | £10.99 | PBS PRICE £8.25

JOHN McAULIFFE: THE KABUL OLYMPICS

The city of Manchester underpins these poems in Fog Lane jogs, Curry Mile cycles, and a moving account of the Manchester Arena bombings, 'City of Trees'. The poet's mind roams beyond to an imagined Kabul, Libya and "The Coast of Nowhere", but these welcome invitations to distant places ("*will we go?... Come on*") only enhance our appreciation of "here"– the song of a blackbird in its "mid-air qualms" or "the end / of a day, brightening."

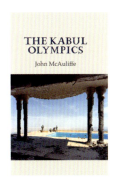

GALLERY PRESS | £10.50 | PBS PRICE £7.88

ABEGAIL MORLEY: THE UNMAPPED WOMAN

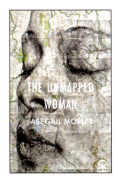

Charting a dark territory of grief and loss, Morley's verse provides the means to navigate depths of utter hopelessness. Her poetry is excellent, each line anticipated breathlessly. This is difficult reading, emotionally harsh and painfully intimate, but *The Unmapped Woman* is ultimately rewarding through the power of its language and unflinching delivery.

NINE ARCHES PRESS | £9.50 | PBS PRICE £7.50

SUMMER BOOK REVIEWS

KATRINA NAOMI: WILD PERSISTENCE

Ranging from the Cornish coastline to Japan, this is a liberating reminder that "there are different ways to live". A fantasy of undressing Billy Collins sits alongside darker poems about attempted rape, the menopause and cancer, but nothing can suppress the wild and quirky energy at play: "I know the secret of broccoli: / It wants to be the drag queen of vegetables". It's hard not to read everything through the lens of our current crisis but *Wild Persistence* is the joyous affirmation we need: "let go of any worry – like the string of a balloon... go on, dance / and look up at the stars".

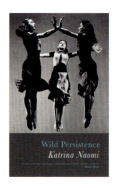

SEREN | £9.99 | PBS PRICE £7.50

JULIE O'CALLAGHAN: MAGNUM MYSTERIUM

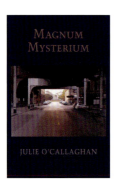

Direct and unpretentious, reading this collection is akin to having a conversation with the poet. Her voice is wry, but compassionate. O'Callaghan draws upon a wealth of life experiences. Many of these, of course, are deeply sad; a portion of this collection considers the passing of her husband. *Magnum Mysterium* therefore becomes a paean to life, and to love – to embracing what you have while it is there, and your memories of what has gone.

BLOODAXE | £10.99 | PBS PRICE £8.25

ARIANA REINES: A SAND BOOK

Totalling over 400 pages, *A Sand Book* is simultaneously weighty and flippant: "& there began my history // Following a bird thru / The sand & its people". Reines mocks the millennial realm where History is "a brand" and questions "why am I trying to talk to you now / In this of all media." Her visionary poems romp through The Dust Bowl to Chopin and unicorn frappuccinos; spanning from Ecbatana to a nail salon in a single breath. Ending with a series of capitalised revelations for our exclamatory age, these shifting sands are far from arid.

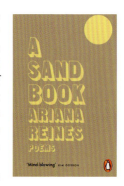

PENGUIN | £12.99 | PBS PRICE £9.75

HEIDI WILLIAMSON: RETURN BY MINOR ROAD

In her mid twenties Heidi Williamson lived in the Scottish community that suffered the terrible tragedy of the Dunblane Primary School shooting. Her third collection, *Return by Minor Road*, revisits this trauma and the slow process of healing. Full of unexpected stillness and beauty, these poems compassionately explore extreme loss and observe how pain can be ingrained onto the landscape itself. This is a heartbreaking sequence, but "regardless, light persists".

BLOODAXE | £9.95 | PBS PRICE £7.47

THESE ARE THE HANDS: NHS ANTHOLOGY

An inspiring anthology which celebrates the dedication of the NHS at this critical time, edited by "The Emergency Poet" Deborah Alma and GP Dr Katie Amiel. Featuring poems by NHS staff alongside donated work by leading poets Michael Rosen, Roger McGough and Wendy Cope, this is an uplifting reminder of our shared humanity. As Michael Rosen claims in the foreword: "the [NHS is the] very heart of who we are and what we are here for." Proceeds from this book support the NHS Charities Together fund.

FAIRACRE PRESS | £9.99 | PBS PRICE £7.50

STAYING ALIVE: REAL POEMS FOR UNREAL TIMES

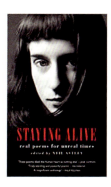

Bloodaxe's monumental trilogy of real poems for unreal times is needed now more than ever. The companion anthologies *Being Alive*, *Staying Alive* and *Being Human* feature poems to suit every mood under the sun in these strange times. Our stand-out favourites include Raymond Carver's "Happiness. It comes on / Unexpectedly" and Derek Mahon's reassuring poem, 'Everything is Going to be All Right'. It's the ideal gift to bring poetic solace, joy or much-needed normality to someone in lockdown.

BLOODAXE | £12.99 | PBS PRICE £9.75

SUMMER PAMPHLETS

CLIVE BIRNIE: PALIMPSEST

In his eighth visual poetry experiment, the Burning Eye Books publisher Clive Birnie uses collage and erasure to give form to everyday ephemera. A quirky character emerges from these fragments, as Palimpsest becomes our anti-superhero, "an underground guru, an elusive philosopher", both gritty and witty: "Palimpsest had a history of addiction / To whisky, prescription drugs and wedding / cake." Words and art, Voodoo and robotics collide with deadpan humour in this joyous palimpsest.

VERVE POETRY PRESS | £7.50 |

OLGA DERMOTT-BOND: APPLE, FALLEN

Dermott-Bond's artful debut pamphlet draws from an esoteric range of subjects to explore ideas of female identity. Herein lies Gaelic mythology, historical artefacts, modern art, and the linguistics of the Navajo people merged seamlessly with personal memoir and reflection. A captivating, thought-provoking collection.

AGAINST THE GRAIN POETRY PRESS | £6.00 |

CAROLE BROMLEY: SODIUM 136

A moving account of the poet's own treatment for "a benign cyst pressing on (the) optic nerve". Bromley bravely documents the journey from poet to patient and celebrates "the unfailing patience and kindness of nurses". Named after the sodium level that the narrator must pass before she can leave hospital, "SODIUM 142. I'm going home," this is a deeply personal poetry of recovery, as well as a timely reminder that "it is good to be alive // it is precious and I must hold it / in my hand like a bird".

CALDER VALLEY POETRY | £7.00 |

NANCY CAMPBELL: NAVIGATIONS

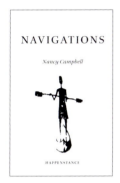

Canal Poet Laureate Nancy Campbell presents "a short story of a long paddle" around various waterways. Canals run throughout these tender tales of boat dwellers, "in all my dreams good and bad I can breathe underwater". Full of gentle humour and playful observations, *Navigations* also tackles the ecological impact of climate change. Ultimately these poems offer a gentler pace of life and a way of navigating through turbulent times: "you'll be surprised just how far you can tip without falling in".

HAPPENSTANCE | £5.00 |

ALI LEWIS: HOTEL

Wonderfully off-kilter, this witty, sometimes dark collection depicts the absurd in the everyday, the sudden upsetting of what is considered normal. A large degree of this is the subject of relationships; of the strains they go under, the ways in which they shift and evolve. Part of this will always, of course, involve the pain of loss and separation, which Lewis portrays sensitively and astutely.

VERVE POETRY PRESS | £7.50 |

NICK ON: ZHOU

Zhou, referring to an ancient Chinese Dynasty as well as the tenth most common surname in mainland China, offers a considered, intricate exploration of Nick On's ancestry and heritage. Here is a meditation on cultural histories, of the passage of time, of the shapes made by lives. Intimate, vivid and compelling, this pamphlet was the well-deserved winner of the 2018/19 Poetry Business International Book and Pamphlet Competition.

POETRY BUSINESS | £6.00 |

SUMMER BOOK LISTINGS

AUTHOR	TITLE	PUBLISHER	RRP
Sascha A. Akhtar	#LoveLikeBlood	Knives Forks Spoons	£12.00
Linda Anderson	The Station Before	Pavilion Poetry	£9.99
John Barnie	Sunglasses	Cinnamon Press	£9.99
Alan Buckley	Touched	HappenStance Press	£10.00
Will Burns	Country Music	Offord Road Books	£10.00
Tim Cresswell	Plastiglomerate	Penned in the Margins	£9.99
Geraldine Clarkson	Monica's Overcoat of Flesh	Nine Arches Press	£9.99
Adam Crothers	The Culture of My Stuff	Carcanet	£9.99
Kwame Dawes / John Kinsella	In the Name of Our Families	Peepal Tree Press	£12.99
Natalie Diaz	Postcolonial Love Poem	Faber & Faber	£10.99
Cath Drake	The Shaking City	Seren	£9.99
Afshan D'souza-Lodhi	re: desire	Burning Eye Books	£9.99
Mike Ferguson	The Lonesomest Sound	Knives Forks Spoons	£10.00
Robert Fitterman	Rob's Word Shop	Ugly Duckling Presse	£24.00
Ella Frears	Shine, Darling	Offord Road Books	£10.00
Charlotte Gann	The Girl who Cried	Happenstance Press	£10.00
David Gilbert	The Rare Bird Recovery Protocol	Cinnamon Press	£9.99
Anna Gurton-Wachter	Utopia Pipe Dream Memory	Ugly Duckling Presse	£15.00
Seán Hewitt	Tongues of Fire	Cape Poetry	£10.00
Wayne-Holloway Smith	Love minus Love	Bloodaxe Books	£10.99
Ranjit Hoskote	The Atlas of Lost Beliefs	Arc Publications	£11.99
Ian House	Just a moment: new and selected poems	Two Rivers Press	£9.99
Rosie Jackson / Graham Burchell	Two Girls and a Beehive	Two Rivers Press	£9.99
Russell Jones	cocoon	Tapsalteerie	£10.00
Peter Kahn	Little Kings	Nine Arches Press	£9.99
Bhanu Kapil	How To Wash A Heart	Pavilion Poetry	£9.99
Stephen Knight	Drizzle Mizzle Downpour Deluge	CB editions	£8.99
Anja Konig	Animal Experiments	Bad Betty Press	£10.00
Theophilus Kwek	Moving House	Carcanet	£10.99
Deborah Landau	Soft Targets	Bloodaxe Books	£10.99
Sadie McCarney	Live Ones	tall-lighthouse	£12.00
Robert Herbert McClean	Songs for Ireland	Prototype	£12.00
Peter McDonald	The Gifts of Fortune	Carcanet	£11.99
Otis Mensah	Safe Metamorphosis	Prototype	£10.00
Abegail Morley	The Unmapped Woman	Nine Arches Press	£9.99
Katrina Naomi	Wild Persistence	Seren	£9.99
Molly Naylor	Stop Trying to be Fantastic	Burning Eye	£9.99
Dalia Neis	Zephyrian Spools: (An Essay, A Wind)	Knives Forks Spoons	£11.00
Grace Nichols	Passport to Here and There	Bloodaxe Books	£9.95
Julie O'Callaghan	Magnum Mysterium	Bloodaxe Books	£10.99
Clover Peake	Beasts & Volcanoes	Knives Forks Spoons	£6.50
Cheryl Pearson	Menagerie	The Emma Press	£10.00
Angela Platt	Crossing the Bloodline	Cinnamon Press	£9.99
Ariana Reines	A Sand Book	Penguin Books	£12.99
Sue Rose	Scion	Cinnamon Press	£9.99
Robert Selby	The Coming-Down Time	Shoestring Press	£10.00
Martha Sprackland	Citadel	Pavilion Poetry	£9.99
Christina Thatcher	How To Carry Fire	Parthian Press	£9.00
Asiya Wadud	Syncope	Ugly Duckling Presse	£14.00
Ahren Warner	The sea is spread and cleaved and furled	Prototype	£12.00
Rory Waterman	Sweet Nothings	Carcanet	£10.99
Rebecca Watts	Red Gloves	Carcanet	£10.99
Mac Wellman	Awe	Ugly Duckling Presse	£13.00
Matthew Welton	Squid Squad	Carcanet Press	£10.99
John Wheway	A Bluebottle in Late October	V. Press	£10.99
Heidi Williamson	Return by Minor Road	Bloodaxe Books	£9.95